19
£4.95

For David, Daniel and Sarah
W.M.

For my father
K.L.

First published 1986 by
Walker Books Ltd
184-192 Drummond Street
London NW1 3HP

Text © 1986 William Mayne
Illustrations © 1986 Kenneth Lilly

First printed 1986
Printed and bound by
L.E.G.O., Vicenza, Italy

British Library Cataloguing in Publication Data
Mayne, William
Come, come to my corner. — (William Mayne's animal library)
I. Title   II. Lilly, Kenneth   III. Series
428.6 PE1119

ISBN 0-7445-0534-8

COME, COME
to my corner

Written by
William Mayne

Illustrated by
Kenneth Lilly

WALKER BOOKS
LONDON

Puss, the wild hare,
comes through the gate at a
corner of the Great Field. It is so big she
cannot see the other side, so big there are
whole hills. The walls go high and straight.

Her black-tipped ears hear the lark
watching from above, his high singing in
the high sky.

'Watch, watch, watch, watch,' the lark sings.
Puss watches. The wind blows in the grass.

'There is danger,' calls another voice. 'Danger, danger,' says the pewit, lapping and clapping his wings as he flies.

'Go back, go back,' say the grouse among the heather shoots. 'Go back.'

'There is nothing here,' says Puss. 'Birds talk to birds.'

She runs along the hare path, and the morning sun warms her ears.

A wise raven walks the crags where the one tree grows among the rocks.

As he flew at dawn he saw the danger in the path. Now he sees Puss coming towards it. Here is something she does not know. Here are sharp teeth waiting.

Raven finds fallen wood from the one tree of the Great Field. He holds a piece and flies with it from the crag, towards Puss as she runs towards him.

The wood pulls him down and down; and can he come to the danger in time? Will he be late, or first hit ground?

At last, when his wings are brushing on stiff rushes, he comes on the danger. There he drops the wood.

The danger bites the wood. It is a springing trap with teeth, where Puss might put her feet, laid in the hare path by a man. It leaps into the air.

Puss jumps and runs. She stretches and she goes away from the movement and the noise.

Raven himself tumbles in the ling, straightens out a feather, sees Puss go, and flies slow up wind to his crag.

'All clear, clear, clear,' sings the lark.

'Welcome, welcome, welcome, welcome,' calls the curlew.

'Careful, careful, careful,' call the pewits, as Puss comes near their nests.

Puss runs a thousand metres across the Great Field, to the far top corner, where wall meets wall at Wilderness.

Here a fox rides the high wall top, coming up slyly from the other side and lying like a stone, watching, waiting.

Puss freezes into stillness beside the grey-green gorse. Overhead the larks sing of danger still.

'I know,' thinks Puss. 'I see fox on the wall top. I shall wait. Fox does not look at me.'

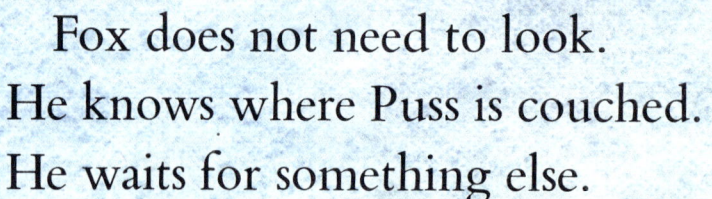

Fox does not need to look.
He knows where Puss is couched.
He waits for something else.

'Careful, careful,' call the ranging pewits.

In another corner of the Great Field a
gate is opened, so far away, so out of sight,
that no message comes to where wall joins
wall at the corner of the Wilderness.

Down at the opened gate a curlew calls,
but she cannot be heard. There is danger
enough where Puss is lying now.

Fox on the wall rests himself down, chin
on his paws, ears picking up the sounds
around him.

Pewits fly low, somewhere beyond Puss.
They shout like gulls, they dive, they
somersault and shriek.

On the wall the fox tightens muscles,
rises on his back legs, licks his lips, ready
for something.

Beyond the gorse bush something treads
on snapping ling, made careless by the birds.
It is the vixen. The dog fox had waited on
the wall, while she came round behind.

Puss bounds up, high on back legs,
gives a clout and a kick on vixen's muzzle,
vaults over dog fox, and goes down the
far wall side.

Foxes follow Puss, to run her down in
the Great Field.

Puss runs up the hill. Ahead of her raven rises out of the way. Behind her the foxes scent her path.

On the hill top she remembers the trap and turns back on her tracks. She waits beside a lonely rock and foxes hurry by the other side.

'I'll leave the Great Field today,' she thinks. 'I'll go down among the hayfields through the far bottom gate.'

No one has told her what came through that gate while the dog fox watched at the high corner.

The foxes can run her down at last, pursuing day and night, tiring her till she can go no further.

The ground, she finds, is silent ahead of her. Everything seems hidden and too still.

She is uneasy. She is running down a cold spring wind, and has no messages from what's in front.

Something is wrong, she knows. She is full of dread.

The ground itself is telling her of danger. She feels it through her feet. She thinks she will find her safety beyond the far bottom gate.

Behind her fox and vixen run, patient and deadly.

But what came through the far bottom gate were the hunters on two feet, their hounds on four.

All are hunting hare. Puss may not go to that corner now.

Hounds call, men shout, all run. Up the slope goes Puss, among the crags, and over the hill top. Hounds follow her.

But not every one. Those that over-ran her scent found the foxes and turned them. The foxes are their quarry now.

Curlews signal like small trumpets, and the hunting men reply with the horn.

Puss can smell new danger far ahead. She cannot turn back, or left, or right. She is surrounded by things she could outrun one at a time, but together are too much.

The danger from ahead is new. It is not the trap the raven sprung for her. She passes that, with wood between its teeth, and smells metal.

Ahead, in the near top corner, something is waiting.

The walls on either side come close, and beyond lies the Wilderness. Beyond that, she thinks, she will run for ever. She sees the stile. She has time to climb it before the hounds reach here.

She has space, she hopes, to get there before the foxes. She sees them cut across the far top corner and come along the wall.

She wishes only that she knew the smell she smells. She puts that from her mind and spurts forward, ten more leaps, nine, eight, and…

…and the stile is filled by something that blocks out the light. It lifts its arms and raises up a shining metal rod. The rod points at Puss. Smoke comes out, and noise.

The man was waiting at the stile for game in the Wilderness. He turned, saw poor Puss come close and closer, and fired his gun on her.

She rolls over and over. There is much noise. Smoke comes out of the gun.

Hounds are yelping down in the Great Field. They came in sight just as the gun was fired, and some have felt the sting of shot, but none are hurt.

Men come up in fury to see what shot their pack.

Foxes slip away behind and down the Great Field.

Birds are silent for a time. The larks fly higher and the deaf world hears nothing. Pewits swirl about the grass; grouse shout and leave the field. The curlew swings his voice up and down. The raven rests on the wind.

Puss should have listened to them all, he thinks.

And Puss has come to her last corner of the Great Field. She saw the gun in time and was not hurt. When the man steps from the stile she goes through, and runs across the Wilderness to the next dale, under the same sky but in safety.